Our Global Community

Farming

Cassie Mayer

Heinemann Library
Chicago, Illinois

Customer Service 888-454-2279
Visit our website at www.heinemannraintree.com

Designed by Joanna Hinton-Malivoire
Photo research by Ruth Smith
Printed and bound in China by South China Printing Co. Ltd.

11 10 09 08 07
10 9 8 7 6 5 4 3 2 1

The Library of Congress has cataloged the first edition of this book as follows:
Mayer, Cassie.
  Farming / Cassie Mayer.
      p. cm. -- (Our global community)
  Includes bibliographical references and index.
  ISBN-13: 978-1-4034-9401-6 (hc)
  ISBN-13: 978-1-4034-9410-8 (pb)
  1. Agriculture--Juvenile literature. I. Title.
  S519.M29 2007
  630'.92--dc22
                            2006034292

Acknowledgements
The publishers would like to thank the following for permission to reproduce photographs: Alamy pp. **7** (Foodfolio), **13** (Sue Wilson); Corbis pp. **4**, **5** (Scott Sinklier), **6** (Stuart Westmorland), **8** (Michael S. Yamashita), **9** (Gary Houlder), **10** (Christine Osborne), **11** (Hein van den Heuvel/zefa), **12** (Ed Young), **14** (Thierry Prat/Sygma), **15** (Alison Wright), **16** (Wolfgang Kaehler), **17** (Margaret Courtney-Clarke), **18** (Randy Wells), **19** (B.S.P.I.), **20** (Keren Su), **21** (aldrin Xhemaj/epa), **22** (Frans Lanting), **23** (Randy Wells; aldrin Xhemaj/epa; Wolfgang Kaehler).

Cover photograph reproduced with permission of Corbis/Keren Su. Back cover photograph reproduced with permission of Corbis/Michael S. Yamashita.

The paper used to print this books comes from sustainable resources.

Contents

Farming Around the World

A farm is where food grows.

A person who farms is a farmer.

What Farmers Grow

wheat

Farmers grow wheat.

We make bread with wheat.

rice

Farmers grow rice.

We eat rice.

bananas

Farmers grow fruit.

apples

We eat fruit.

radishes

Farmers grow vegetables.

We eat vegetables.

What Farmers Raise

Farmers raise cows.

We drink milk from cows.

wool

Farmers raise sheep.

wool

We use wool from sheep.

How Farmers Work the Land

Farmers use big machines to work the land.

Farmers use small machines to work the land.

Farmers use animals to work the land.

Farmers use tools to work the land.

Farmers use the land to grow food.

Farmers are important to everyone.

Picture Glossary

 **machine** object that helps you do something. Machines make work easier.

 **tool** object that you use with your hands. Tools make work easier. Tools can be smaller than machines.

 **wool** fur of a sheep. We use wool to make sweaters.

Index

Note to Parents and Teachers

This series expands children's horizons beyond their neighborhoods to show that communities around the world share similar features and rituals of daily life. The text has been chosen with the advice of a literacy expert to ensure that beginners can read the books independently or with moderate support. Stunning photographs visually support the text while engaging students with the material.

You can support children's nonfiction literacy skills by helping students use the table of contents, headings, picture glossary, and index.

DISCAR**DED**

DEMCO